THE GOLDEN BOOK OF THE SANCTITY

By
Father John Doe
(Rev. Ralph Pfau)
Author
of
SOBRIETY AND BEYOND
SOBRIETY WITHOUT END

* * *

The SMT Guild, Inc.
P.O. Box 313
Indianapolis, IN 46206

Hazelden Publishing
Center City, Minnesota 55012-0176
hazelden.org/bookstore

© 1967 by Hazelden Foundation. First published 1967
by SMT Guild, Inc., Indianapolis. First published by Hazelden 1998
All rights reserved
Printed in the United States of America
No portion of this publication may be
reproduced in any manner without the
written permission of the publisher

ISBN: 978-1-56838-575-4

"Me a Saint?
You know I ain't—
And could never, never be:
What's that you say?
'A man approved'?
Today!
By God;
Not men
Or even me!
No matter what I am;
Or will ever, ever be? You mean that I.........."

Well, let's read on
And really see;
What is truly meant
By *sanctity* ......

*O Lord, make me a part of the answer
instead of a part of the problem; use me,
O God, just as I am today, but above
everything else, make me willing—No
matter what You make of me, or what
You may permit my sins to make of me!*

SANCTITY

Today the word *'spiritual'* and *'sanctity'* are almost 'bad' words. Many shy away from even mentioning the terms. And most people seem to be horrified at the idea that they could even think of ever being a saint. And almost inevitably one gets the reply to the mention of such a possibility: "Me, a saint?! That's ridiculous!"

Even in the A.A. Book we find the statement used: "We are not saints." But the Big Book does very aptly qualify this with "We are willing to grow along spiritual lines." And as we shall see as we go along the route to sanctity that it is in the misunderstanding of these terminologies that make so many shy away from such terms as 'spiritual' and 'saint.' It is also the reason that so many members shy away from the so-called 'spiritual side' of the program, or have so much unnecessary difficulties with the spiritual life—they have a completely distorted idea of what spiritual life and sanctity really mean.

Perhaps it will be a good idea to re-state here what we said in our very first Golden Book[1] about spirituality and sanctity and many of the reasons which are responsible for wrong conceptions of their true meaning:

"Many have difficulty with the spiritual side of the program because they have a distorted idea of what is meant by the term 'spiritual.' To many, such a term conjures up in their minds innumerable prayers, a long face, isolation *in*human qualities of human associate, a retreating gait, somber groanings, and what-have-you.

---

[1] *The Golden Book of the Spiritual Side.*

Nothing could be farther from the truth. A spiritual person is one who does *what* he has to do, *when* he has to do it, in the *best* way he can do it and who *expects* and *gets* the guidance, the strength, and the success from God through humble prayer and meditation. They realize that whether they pray or eat or work or play or sleep, they do it all for the honor and glory of God and thus praise God in doing His Will."

Or as one recent spiritual writer expresses this truth very succinctly: "Even if it bores *you* to death to pray; pray anyway because it *pleases God.*"

So let's try to answer two very relevant questions:

1) What is sanctity.

2) What does God want us to do.

There have been literally thousands of books written on what is sanctity. Many good; many bad; most confusing, indefinite and regulatory *ad infinitum*.

In answer to the second question there can be no doubt just what God expects of us. He tells us over and over again: "Be perfect." Therefore there can be no doubt that also He does expect perfection in us—that He expects sanctity of everyone, for perfection is sanctity. But just what is precisely this *perfection*, this *sanctity* which He demands. And we know that He is obligated to lavish the means of attaining to it, since we are here in this world by His choice, not by our own. So, just as a parent who begets or adopts a child is responsible to that child, so Almighty God who has adopted us *all* as His children is responsible to us to see to it that we have all the things we need to fulfill His command: *Be perfect.* And here He also in so commanding expects sanctity in us all—*His* children.

But specifically, just what is this sanctity, this perfection He expects—in fact demands of all? Does it mean that God expects all of us to reach a stage wherein everything is virtue, and nothing is sin? Does it mean that we are all expected to reach that state of perfection wherein there is only good, and no evil? Does it mean that He demands that we all reach that state wherein our every act is perfect? Perhaps—in eternity! But we are not in eternity—we are very earth bound as yet. So, just what does sanctity consist of here and now?

We feel that a much simpler idea of sanctity than that which is contained in many spiritual books is a very necessary thing for most of us. We feel that putting sanctity in its true perspective will not only enable the average John Doe to understand it, but also that he will endeavor to attain to it, not as something ethereal and out of this world with its 'halo' shielding it from most of us, but something real—and practical—and attainable by *everyone* without exception.

We will endeavor in our own stumbling way to do this. It will be a little bit 'different' from the average explanation and approach to sanctity, to perfection, and to God; it will be even at bit "unique;" but an attempt will be made to keep it simple, and it will be, we sincerely hope, valid, orthodox and perhaps bring many readers at least to the starting line leading to the spiritual life, to sanctity and to God.

Perhaps our explanation of sanctity may be somewhat like the incident which we experienced some years back. It was in a small midwestern town and we were attending a banquet of the Knights of Columbus—a Catholic fraternal organization. Seated next to me was the Abbot of a nearby newly founded Trappist Monastery. And usually Abbots of Trappist Monasteries did not go around attending banquets. We mentioned this fact to him. "Yes it is unusual," he said. "In fact, as far as I know it is probably the first time it has ever happened." And then he slyly added: "And when Rome finds it out it may be the last time!"

So we will give our idea of what sanctity means, and what God means when He says "Be you perfect"—it may be the first time ever expressed just in this way, but then, it also may be the last time too—verbally or in writing! But it is merely our own opinion, as is everything in A.A. And you know something? Even with the thousands of "screwy" opinions voiced about various things in A.A. they work. They really do!

We like to divide *sanctity* into three kinds or qualities:

1) *Heroic sanctity*—in which classification we find such stalwart men and women of history as St. Paul, the Apostles, the Martyrs, and the like: all of whom accomplished great deeds perfectly both in view of God and man. They were outstanding individuals chosen by God for outstanding public deeds. Theirs were very special vocations, chosen specifically by God for a specific work in an heroic manner and at the same time were public figures in history's annals. We may possibly here or there imitate some of their virtue in kind, but never in their heroic quality. No one is ever expected to do so, unless called explicitly by God as they were. We are never sure, of course, but we do not think He has rung your phone as yet! We admire them; we venerate them; we applaud them and the grace of God which accomplished such great things through them, but we can never identify with them in kind. They practiced *heroic sanctity*.

2) *Solemn sanctity*—In this class we find the long list of *canonized saints*. These were the men and women of history who performed eventually through the call and grace of God heroic virtue but did not accomplish outstanding tasks or deeds in public life. However all the saints did whatever they had to do—perfectly. St. Therese of Lisieux in her own autobiography emphasized the fact that *great deeds are not necessary* to qualify for heroic virtue—perfection in simple daily life also takes heroism—a special vocation. She simply did *all things* each day in her ordinary life—as a Nun—perfectly. She was canonized. She proved that heroic virtue worthy of solemn canonization can be in very simple and ordinary deeds done perfectly because it is God's Will. Her sanctity and all the other canonized saints also were recipients of a very special grace and vocation. These too we admire, we venerate, we applaud them and the grace of God which accomplished such perfection in them albeit simple. But again we can not expect to identify with them without a specific vocation. They practiced heroic virtue, and thereby were deemed worthy of solemn sanctity: canonization.

3) *Simple sanctity*—Here we find or should find the rest of the vast human race—you and you and you and me! It is not a *special* vocation, it is a universal vocation to all mankind—to be saints, to be perfect.

What does this really mean? It means first and foremost that we must *accept ourselves as we are—today*: good or bad, sinner or saint, ignorant or educated, screwball, or alcoholic (or both), or rich, or poor, Catholic, Protestant, Jew, agnostic, single, married, working, or out of work—and on and on: *exactly whatever we are now*. Then we do the best we can to *fit in* this place in life as we *are—with what we have*, not what some pious theorist tells what we *ought* to be or have. Let us never forget that one thing sanctity is *not—*it is *never objective*. This is precisely the error made by many spiritual writers. "To be a saint," they tell us, "we must do this and that and follow this rule and that and obey this law and that—perfectly."

Far be it from us to discredit the value of rules, and regulations and laws as in the extreme views of those who criticize authoritarianism. But all rules and regulations and laws—human or Divine are to be obeyed *in so far as one is capable of so doing*, and according to God's Providence. The old Romans used to say "Omnes leges secundum capacitatem." (All laws are to be obeyed according to the capability of the individual.) Again, this is not objective, but subjective. They say: "Facientem quod est in se, Deus non deneget gratiam." This means "Whoever does what in him lies, God will *not* deny the grace" to *will*, not necessarily to accomplish!

Therefore the perfection which God expects is in the willing, not in the fulfillment. And we may be surprised on judgment day to find many whom we looked upon as big sinners in this old world, as saints in eternity. "Peace on earth to men of *good* will."

Perhaps we will better understand this whole idea of sanctity by using the term *sanctio* (sanction) rather than *sanctus* (holy, saintly). *Sanctus* is used referring to God. He is *holy*—all holy. But anyone who has the *approval*, the *sanction* of God *today* is a saint, and either has or is on the road to *sanctity*—"a man approved!"—by God, not men, nor you, nor me!

Therefore, in order to start on this road, one must be a *good sinner*. This means that one must *admit* that he *is* a sinner. We must admit and accept ourselves as we are, and then be *ready* to *fit in*. God will do the rest, in his time and His way.

This is the basis for the first and most necessary of the virtues: humility. It is the first step of A.A. : "We admitted we were powerless over alcohol; that our lives were unmanageable." It is emphasized in each of the subsequent steps of the program, as we shall later on see—i.e. the inventory; steps 4, 5, 6; and the chapter in the A.A. Book on "How It Works" and "Into Action." For after all this whole idea of adjustment to life, to God's Will, to His approval, His sanction—to sanctity is nothing more nor less than a mixture of three basic ingredients: weakness + willingness + grace. The first and the latter are always there—we go in the middle. So, don't stumble over number 1. "The weak ones of this world God has chosen to confound the strong."

Lest we be like the little boy who went to confession and said: "Bless me God, I *forgot* my sins!"

So it is that the A.A. Book says "we are not saints we are *willing* to grow along spiritual lines." This does not deny that *sanctity* is the final *aim*. Right now we are seeking God's approval, His sanction: whatever we are. He will make the saint—in His own time, and in His own way—here or hereafter.

Again, back to step number 1. We have become *honest*, we are big sinners, *but* having humbly admitted it, we have God's approval, His sanction—and behold the paradox of paradoxes: the *sinner saint*!

We have just joined the *Sinners Club:*"

No officers; No meetings; No dues;

Just a daily prayer;

"O God be merciful to me a sinner."

We have taken the first step in obtaining the *sanction* of God, we begin to be saints—we begin to fit in life and Providence, just as we are, with no excuses like the little girl used when she told her mother that her brother broke her doll.

"How did he do it, honey?" queried the mother.

"I hit him over the head with it!" whimpered the little girl!

Speaking of this *fitting* in just as we are, we must realize that although all are born "free and equal"—this refers to *rights*: legal and eternal. But it does not mean that all are psychologically or *physically* or *mentally* equal. We are all a little different. And this must be understood clearly if we wish to fully understand the Providence of God and the question of *being perfect*, and of sanctity. We hope this will vividly demonstrate why it is that we say that perfection, sanctity, is never *objective*. It is not a matter of perfect objective adherence to the Laws of God and of the spiritual life; but it is in the *willingness* to aim and try to adjust to God's will *for us*, beginning with that particular type personality and character with which He has endowed us. This alone will explain the mystery of *"Be you perfect,"* which is telling us "be what *I* have willed you to be." Fit in My Providence with that which I gave you, whatever that personality may be."

And here we find many types. And if we pictorialize it a bit, it will show the seeming inequality and the ease with which some seem to adjust while others find such difficulty. But if we remember willingness is perfection, there will be *no* real inequality. It will also give every alcoholic and many, many others in life a bit more hope, and perhaps faith, and confidence—every joy. As long as we bear in mind: Sanctity, perfection, is having the sanction of God—not perfection of actions.

On the following pages we have a series of eight figures, each one expressing a type of *person*. There are of course many, many shades more, but these will suffice to emphasize the fact that *sanctity* is *sanction*—not of all men and women, nor of you, nor of me: but only of *God*: today!

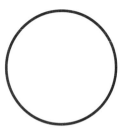

The *round* individual. This person is very normal, and will have little difficulty *'fitting in.'* The place for this person in life is the most frequently found. *"A round peg in a round hole."*

Here we have the *square* one. This individual will find it a lot more difficult to find the *square* hole and will not fit in a *round* one. He or she must find the square one, or at least be willing.

The *angular* personality: Still more 'unique' than the two first ones, and also it will be more difficult for this person to find a fit. He or she may even fail because of this, but what did we say: "Not perfection of action, but of willingness!"

Behold the *egghead*.[1] Getting more common, but we wonder whether the 'holes' of that shape are growing apace! In any case, it will be still more difficult for this character. And once again, we repeat and repeat and repeat: *"It is willingness."*

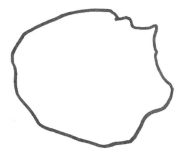

The *alcoholic*! This individual is in for a very rough time. A lot cutting-off rough edges is necessary to find a fit. But what was it? *Willingness, willingness, willingness!* And some 300,000 have rubbed off a lot of edges! Or at least are willing.

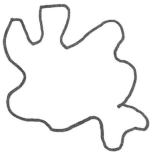

The *alcoholic neurotic*. Still more rough edges. Still more difficulties in cutting. But still whole, still rational, and once again we call out to all: *it's willingness, willingness, willingness!*

---

[1] Just what do we mean by *egghead*? Your interpretation is as good as any!

The *psychoneurotic*. There will be a lot of broken and bruised parts along the way of life. But there is a fit—in the Will and Providence of God. And if it fits there and if there is union of wills—the human and the Divine. There is *sanction*!

Here we see the *psychopathic* personality—there is already a *break* of reason. There is no freedom of human will. *But there is freedom of Divine Will!* And, between you and me, we are going to look for them in the *upper* tier, up there—in eternity!

The preceding *figures* were used to demonstrate more realistically what we mean when we say that *sanctity* is *subjective*—which is again the willingness to adjust to life and God's Will *for us*. His Will already has been 'adjusted' to us from all eternity.

So, whatever figure may point to us, we must fit in whether we like it or not. And we feel most of our readers being alcoholics will find themselves either in figure 5 or 6—or who knows maybe a number 1 will be reading this. We still must all fit in as we are to what God has willed for us, willingly or unwillingly. It is true we have a free will, but in certain applications in the life of an individual personality, there is only one way—or else! What do we read in the big A.A. Book: "We all reached the point where there were three choices left: sobriety, insanity or death." So these "marks" are indelible. How do we adjust? How do any of the above achieve *sanctity*? *Simply* seek the Will of God for *us*! As we are today!

Everyone in life is obligated to find his or her own adjustment. In A.A. we *work the program*—the twelve steps. And one by one they lead *up*; they lead us *up*, to God's Will as we read in step 11; "...praying only for knowledge of His will for us and the power to carry that out." This is exactly repressive of what we have been describing about sanctity being subjective. And we shall see when we come to that step—that is sanctity, for we have achieved God's approval, His *sanction, for us*.

It is the story of every soul. Sometime, somewhere, they all reach the moment of truth. It matters not what 'type' they are. Not only the alcoholic, but the heroic saints, all of them had their moment of truth. And the heroic *saint*, seeking the approval and sanction of God asked, and then carried out the answer of "Lord what will you have me to do?" "Seeking knowledge of His Will *for us* and the power to carry it out." Paul asked it; Mary Magdalen asked it; Peter asked it—but these great men and women asked it once and for all. WE alcoholics are the kind who must seek it one day at a time. "...praying only for knowledge of His will for us and the power to carry that out"--today we are seeking God's *approval*, His *sanction* today!

Sanctity has nothing to do with religion "per se." It has only to do with the Will of God for us; with God's approval, God's sanction of us—today.

This idea can and should be carried into every area of our living. Let's take a look:

1) *In our homes*—family. Whether we are the father or the mother; whether we have a wife or no wife; a husband or no husband; children or no children; fine house or just a shack; or an apartment; or even a tent. The real question is: "Does God *approve, sanction* us today?" Not does anyone else approve—but does *God approve*? If He does, we find sanctity in the home. How can we know whether God

approves? All we have to do is to ask our conscience—*honestly*.

2) *Our Job*. Whether we have a good or poor job; or no job; an easy or a difficult job; or own our own business—"Does God *approve?*" Have we *His* sanction? Sanctity is sanction!

3) *In our social life*. We may have many friends or few friends; close friends or transient friends; or even no friends or enemies (Christ did!). Does God approve our attitudes and behavior towards them all, friends or enemies? Do we have *His* sanction? Well, sanctity is sanction!

4) *Our thought life*. Whether we have good thoughts, or bad thoughts or indifferent thoughts—or *no* thoughts! (It is said that some people 'set' all day and think; while others just 'set'!) The *kind* of thoughts which pass through our minds and imaginations mean nothing. The big question is "Does God approve our attitude toward them?" Do the thoughts have His *sanction*, or does our will's reaction to the thoughts have His sanction? The kind of thoughts mean nothing. Our attitude toward them and what we do about them means everything. Has this His approval, His sanction? Sanction is sanctity.

5) *In our financial affairs*. We may have a little money or we may have a lot a money; we may get a big salary or a small salary or income; or we may even have no money. Does God approve my attitude toward and the handling of it today? Approval is sanction, and sanction is—what was that word?—sanctity.

6) *Our moral lives*. We may have committed lots of sins or few sins; (No one has committed *no* sins!) lots of big sins or a few big sins; lots of little sins or a few little sins; maybe no big sins (In A.A.!?)

Let us remember again, sanctity, simple sanctity, does *not* exclude sins—not even big ones. The big question is what is our sincere will towards sins? Many theologians in fact hold that there is such a thing as a *cross* of sin. These are the ones who try and try and try and try and fail—again and again and again. They *may* be carrying *a cross of sin*—which is the nearest to the one Christ carried: we our own sins: He the world's sins! So when we see the slipper, the seeming *big* sinner, the recidivist (repeater), yes even the public sinner—let us never, *never* judge, for what is it A.A. teaches us: "There but for the grace of God go I!" And who knows? Who really knows, just whom has God's *approval*, permissive Providence? Not men, nor you, nor me—but only *God!* Does He approve, has He sanctioned this whole affair? Well, let's be honest He *did* approve, by *permitting*, just lots of big sins in the life of Mary Magdalen—and Paul who *hated* the Christians as Saul—and Peter, who denied Him—and on and on and on up to that man or woman we point our finger at and whisper: *unclean!* Let us not deceive ourselves, sanctity is sanction, and that guy or gal may be, just *may* be on the way to becoming another Mary Magdalen, or Paul, or Peter lugging the *cross of sin* now, but willingly. Sanction is sanctity. Not sanction of sin, but sanction of the sinner who is *willing*. After all the Holy Spirit breathes where He will—and when He wills—in the total Providence of God, setting up of in detail the foundation in humanity for eternity God's own masterpiece: the saints in eternity with all the darks and lights; the highlights and the shadows; the smooth, the brilliant, and the deep dark caverns on which He, the Divine artist, paints and paints and paints—you and you and you and me!

7) *Now the spiritual life.* Do we say lots of prayers, or a few prayers, or no prayers; do we make many sacrifices, or only a few sacrifices or no sacrifices—today? It does not now matter for if it be part of God's overall plan, if it be His will, eventually we will be very prayerful. The question again is does God approve today's spiritual life? Does our spiritual life have His sanction, His approval? *Sanctity*—today!

8) *Then there are our emotions.* Everyone has emotions, nerves. Some have strong ones, others have weak ones—it makes no difference. We may get angry, or we may not get angry (very often!). We may be very placid, elated, agitated, irritated, fearful, courageous, crying, jittery, or what have you. All these may be true emotions; or they may all be just 'feelings,' it all makes no difference, does God approve? We can never judge the other one, particularly in the world of emotions or feelings—but God can—and does. Again, does He approve? Does He perhaps *sanctify* these things? His sanction is sanctity!

9) *In our A.A. Life.* Do we have lots of slips, a few slips, no slips?

Do we make many twelfth step calls, a few such calls, or perhaps no such calls? Do we go to many meetings, a few meetings—no meetings?

It all matters little. What matters very much though is does God approve *our* A.A. for *us*? For God's sanction is everything—is sanctity. It is *His* approval which counts, not our own, nor others.

However God does use a guide, an advisor—a sponsor very often to *express* His approval through them. This will avoid misjudging our own *prowess*, our own ability, our own progress and capabilities. These are usually irrelevant to sanctity, and as sanctity, are *always subjective*. Or as the Dad told his boy who was bragging about winning the 100 yard, then the mile race: "That surely is fine lad, but never forget if it was against a jackass you would have lost every time!"

So in A.A. (and in all spiritual life) we seek advice—*not agreement*. Many people go to person after person after person for "advice" *until* they find someone to *agree* with *them*.

One big danger in the spiritual life and seeking sanctity, we want too much, too quick! Why is this dangerous? Because if we reached 'objective' sanctity too suddenly, there would be no place to go but *down*. That is why we must seek advice and not concentrate on trying to be "objective" saints—but only the approval of our lives *today*, whatever they may be or have been *today*—by God, not men, nor us, only the sanction of God. That is sanctity.

However we can concentrate on being good *objective* sinners every day, for then there is no place to go but *up!* Up the Twelve Steps.

So let's take them one at a time along the road to sanctity to reach a happy sobriety with God's approval, with His sanction—with *His sanctity*.

THE TWELVE STEPS TO SANCTITY

1. *We admitted we were powerless over alcohol—that our lives were unmanageable.*

Our very first statement in the Twelve Steps, we note, is an *admission* of our own powerlessness; that our very lives have become *unmanageable*. Being an alcoholic and powerless over alcohol so that our lives are "bottoms up" does not *in itself* indicate a sinner, or sin. Let us never forget that *alcoholism is a disease*. An alcoholic—one who is powerless over alcohol, whose life is unmanageable, is a very *sick* person. We should never for a moment forget this. If the new guy or gal does, he or she may fail the program. However the odds are very high that he or she is also quite a sinner—something which may or may not be mixed up with the person's alcoholism.

So we are *powerless*, and we really mean it. We are unmanageable in our lives, and we really mean it. If this is true, then *God approves, sanctions* it for being God, He can not very well deny truth.

Now comes the paradox again—the sinner-saint! We in this first step are powerless, our lives are unmanageable, and without a doubt we are also sinners, and probably big ones! But in making this admission—today—we have the approval of God. We have His *sanction*. And sanction is sanctity!

Read on!

We hear objections. How can such a person ever make himself *worthy* of God? Who's kidding whom? Who ever *made themselves* worthy of God! Always, and everywhere, and with everyone; the very first step to God is to *admit* our unworthiness! What use has God for a *worthy* person? They do not need Him. But the alcoholic, the powerless one, the unmanageable one, the *unworthy* one not only needs God, but needs Him absolutely. This is why since the beginning, without exception, the powerless ones, the weak ones, the unmanageable ones, the sinners, the failures, the sick, and the blind and the lame and the alcoholics—all:

2. *Came to believe that a Power greater than themselves could restore them to sanity.* And may we interpolate a bit?—and to *sanctity*! With His *approval*, with His *sanction.*

Why the term "Power greater than ourselves?" Many are confused by this and ask why not use the term *God*?

The reason is quite simple. Many, many who come to A.A. have no idea of God. Alcohol is no respecter of persons. And the program of A.A. is open to *all*—Christians, Jews, agnostics, atheists, even to Mao Tsung should he be an alcoholic! They need help—and must accept a Power greater than themselves—the idea of a power—any subjective idea that they have *honestly*. To ask and demand they accept the orthodox idea of God at this juncture would be foolhardy. Even in step two, and throughout the program, the term "God *as we understood Him"* is used. Why? Because again, each one can *only* accept God as he *honestly* in his conscience understands Him. It is all he has. It is God. And you know something, *God* approves, and gives His sanction, because it was He who first gave each one the belief he or she has. Faith is a *gift*—and given or withheld from each. He gives both the quantity and quality. It is true that reason leads to faith, to God, *but* it is God who guides that reason which has found Him, in just so far as He wills. This He approves. This He sanctions. And regardless of the quality, or amount, or depth of the faith; or of the subjective idea the individual has honestly of a Power greater than himself, if he *"came to believe"*—he has God's sanction *today*. Sanctity in an agnostic? Hmmmmmmm, could be! You know there *are* Christians and Jews and believers of all sorts who are still very, very big sinners! Faith cannot be bought. Faith cannot be forced. Faith cannot be the measuring rod. It is a *gift*—in quantity, in quality, and in depth. So whatever be the quantity, or the quality, or the depth or the lack of faith we may have today—let's be one who has:

3) *Made a decision to turn our will and our lives over to the care of God as we understood Him.*

We turn them over just as they are—today. It may very well be possible that our will is not very willing today. We may be very hesitant, or rebellious, or resentful, or full of self pity. But let's turn it over to *Him* so *He* will be able to remove the hesitancy, the resentment, the rebellion, the self pity, or what have you. This, by the very fact of turning our will over to Him will obtain His *approval*, His *sanction*. It is the *only* will *we* have, today. Give it to *Him as it is* therefore then as we learned in the first and second step, He will not only restore us to sanity, give us power, manage our lives, but will also *"clean up our will"* so that we can become willing, completely willing—and with that comes complete approval and sanction. And what have we been saying over and over again: *Sanctity is sanction.* We aim our will at God as is; He strengthens and remakes it; they *join* to each other—the human and the Divine. That is perfection, that is sanction, that is approval, that is sanctity; *the union of wills*, not the perfection of action!

"The union of wills"—a phrase we will use again and again, because to repeat right now—the union of wills, the human and the Divine, *is* perfection; the only true perfection; the only true sanctity. For what does it profit a man if he perfect every action of life according to the law, if he does not have the approval of God; if his will and the Divine will run contrary the one to the other? Well, what does it profit? So, let's turn ours over to *Him today* no matter what condition it has fallen into.

And throw in our lives too. They may also be very messy, but again it is the only life we have—just like our will. So let's not even right now take a look at the awful mess; let's take a good look at God *as we understand Him*, i.e. your *honest* conviction of God for *you*. He *will*, as we mentioned in the step above, restore us to sanity—and we shall have His *approval*, His *sanction: today*. Then *He* will help us with our step four and we will be convinced that He approves it.

4) *Made a searching and fearless moral inventory of ourselves.*

We make this inventory searching and fearless with the knowledge now that He wants us to and therefore, as we said, approves, and sanctions it regardless of its contents! This inventory should take away all guilt—we are *not guilty*. God asks us to take an inventory for *forgiving*, totally—not for condemning. Hence, we have *no* guilt. We had *responsibility*! and we *will* have the responsibility of doing what we can beginning today: but no guilt *please*! Sorrow, yes; but this is an act of the *will*, and God approves; but *guilt, no;* this is feeling, self pity, regret, etc., and all the *destructive* attitudes towards ourselves. This God does not approve. Remember again it is willingness, willingness, willingness—and guilt is never in the will. Guilt in its two meanings exist only in the emotions or in judgment. Let's have neither lest we be our severest judge and blind us to God—His mercy, His love, His will and willingness to forgive. Then in Step Five we will without regrets, or guilt, or remorse be one who, gladly though perhaps with difficulty, sought out someone and:

5) *Admitted to God, to ourselves, and to another human being the exact nature of our wrongs.*

Our admission to God gains His *approval and sanction*; our admission to ourselves (honestly) makes us willing; and our admission to another human being clarifies and permits this third party to join our will with God's as to the past, the present, and the future aims. We learn much about God and His will for us in A.A. from this sponsor, or advisor, or friend. He has been through it all, including step five. And our conviction is that as God sees us there together—one admitting and the other listening and advising. He approves with a very, big, broad smile. Both have His sanction, both have His approval, and perfection? What did He say about it through Paul: "Charity is the *bond* of perfection." And in the fifth step we have charity at work in reality and in truth. Approval—sanction—*perfection*.

We mentioned that God smiles. Does God smile? Well far be it from us to go into the theology of it. Your opinion is as good as mine. But we feel quite sure that He *must* have a sense of humor. For to have created all of us in the world, with all of our eccentricities and differences and peculiarities—just as you and we have for His greater honor and glory—*He had to have a sense of humor!* And how can anyone with a sense of humor not smile, at least once in a while. In fact we believe that He smiles quite often as some of the things we in our small imaginations make such big issues out of. But that is only our opinion. But it might be a very good opinion to take along on your fifth step!

The "wrongs" we admit—does God approve them? Not precisely— He did *permit* them; and He certainly approves your telling and admitting them to Him, yourself, and another human being with a smile! Then you will see it was much easier for us and that we:

6) *Were entirely ready to have God remove all those defects of character.*

"*Ready* and willing." And if we are ready and willing, then we can be sure that He also is ready and willing to do it, and that automatically is His approval; His *sanction*. (In case you should happen to wonder, we are watching a *saint* being assembled—out of a mess of rubble!) So, read on.

Let's for a moment go back to the eight "figures" we saw in the beginning of this booklet. Remember? The "bumps," the "irregular lines," the "rough spots"?

Well, here we say to Him: "And now, dear God you fit us in—for evidently we have not yet found our niche. Maybe we will find it in A.A. In fact I know we will if we are willing, for we are no longer going to try to "fit in." From now on we are *ready* and willing for *You* to do it—in *Your* way. Then we will know our niche, and You having fitted us to it, we will have *Your* approval, *Your* sanction, and *Your* will. And all we will have to do from now on 'one day at a time' will be, as we shall have at least the *good* will to do, in Step eleven, to be joined to *Your* will." Sanction? Approval? Perfection? Never forget, we said we would mention it over and over and over again: "Perfection is in the union of wills; not in the perfection of actions!" And we will have, in the next step, have:

7) *Humbly ask Him to remove our shortcomings.*

Since God does usually act in His time and in His way—He ordinarily does not act precipitously—*right now*. He lets us *grow* as He permits all nature to grow. That is why the A.A. Book says "We are willing to *grow*...." Therefore He does not remove our defects of character *right now*. He will *"erase"* them: gradually, like all erasing! So, since we shall have many of these defects left for a long time—maybe even until eternity!—they will cause "shortcomings." We must expect them; we must accept them; we must humbly ask Him to remove them in His time and in His way. But, you know something, pal? If He *permits* them to remain in spite of our request, prayers and efforts; He does approve: we *do* have *His* sanction, in spite of them. Remember Paul? "The good that I will, I do not; the evil I detest and will not, that I do!" What will release him? He tells us: "The grace of God." And do you want to know when He will begin to remove them? On the day we reach that first word in Step seven in our lives: *"humbly"* ask *Him*. For "humility" is the one act, the one virtue, the one fact in human life which brings quick approval; quick sanction.

Remember the story in the Scriptures about the Pharisee and the Publican? They both went up to the Temple to pray. And the Pharisee stood way up front, and stood "way"—up! Then he enumerated all of his virtues, how he gave to the poor; how he gave tithes to the Temple, very *"humbly"* (?) and undoubtedly very loudly, although the Scriptures do not mention it. But we feel he was also looking out the back side of his eye on that *"critter"* in the rear—he then exclaimed for all to hear: "Thank God I am not like the rest of men, like that Publican—he even smells bad." (The scriptures left those last four words out too!)

Then the Publican—poor, disheveled by his work, and with head bowed, "not even daring to lift his eyes to Heaven" softly, but humbly and with much reverential love of God, said: "O God, be merciful to me a sinner!" (Joined the sinner's club?)!

The scriptures then brings out the true relationship between God and man and sin and virtue and justification and sanctity. "The Publican returned to his house justified rather than the Pharisee."

What was that? The Publican had obtained God's *approval, His sanction*—not men's, nor his, nor yours, nor mine—but *God's*: sanction is sanctity.

He was absolutely *honest*, he was absolutely *humble*—he was justified; sanctified. He had become *"a man approved"*—by *God*, not men nor by the Pharisee, nor anyone but *God*: and with that approval in his humility was given birth to sanctity—through the grace of God in spite of the condemnation of men. How about you? With this picture in our memory it will be easy to have:

8) *Made a list of all persons we had harmed, and became willing to make amends to them all.*

In this step we see at work that "charity" which is the bond of perfection; and the *willingness* which is the *aim* of perfection.

When we, in the first and second steps, admitted the need for help and were *willing* to let a Power greater than ourselves—(God as we understood Him)—take over the restoring of us to sanity and sobriety, we learned also that our *willingness* had opened the door to sanctity. Being completely willing, made our aim toward sanctity *true*.

In step eight we find many great defects from our past living. And we also know "darn" well that we, being virtually bankrupt in all of our areas of living, could not immediately make up the harm we had done to so many. But again here as we have pointed out in our read pages—perfection. Sanctity is not made up from *actions* of perfection but from *willingness*.

So we are "willing to make amends to them all," and in the next step we will see that *"all"* is still only our *aim*, our *willingness*, not necessarily our accomplishment. Probably, most A.A.'s will never be able to make amends to them *"all,"* because charity, which is the "bond" of perfection, the *"seal"* of sanctity, will prevent us from making some of the amends, less in the doing, we injure *others*. This is the charity which we are told *binds* perfection. So it is that in step nine we

9) *Made direct amends to people wherever possible, except when to do so would injure them or others.*

Note what we just pointed out above: "Made direct amends… except when to do so would injure them or others." We are obligated by the law of charity, by the love of our neighbor to omit *amends* whenever making them will injure them or others. We do not take into consideration *our* own selves but "them or others."

In these instances we simply omit them; and we ask God to make the amends for us. Many times this is very much more difficult we think. The leaving of the amends to God demands on our part *trust* in Him; and a deep *humility* in ourselves since we will never be 'sure' that they are made, except by faith in Him and His love and in His ability to do so. We find ourselves saying to ourselves and others: "I wish I *could* make these particular amends." This is pride whereas, humility tells us "we can't, God will."

Once more it is the *willingness* on our part to let Him do so with a deep faith and trust that He will. He, through His law of love, the law of charity to our fellowmen, asks that we do it this way. And when we do it in this way, then He has approved, He has *sanctioned* what we have done.

Re-read this step. Note how good God is. Particularly note how simple He makes it for us. He does not say "You must make every little amend to everyone without exception or—else!" He only asks that we do so: wherever possible, when it won't hurt others.

Did we hear someone remark that God did not write these steps? Well, maybe He did not, but he did use those early members of A.A. who did write them as 'instruments' to bring His message to us alcoholics. And let us never forget one factor of life: "God will *use* us if we let Him; but He does not need us."

So now let's travel on up the three steps, and see how He will *use us*—if we let Him—or if we are willing. He approves, but the big question is, will we approve? If we do, then we are willing, and we will certainly have His *approval*, His *sanction*. And in all the repetitive steps: the 'inventory' in ten; and the "prayer" in eleven; and the "carrying the message" in twelve, we will be "approved" each day, one day at a time. Approval of God, not men or women, nor us—*sanction, sanctity!*

10) Continued to take personal inventory and when we wrong promptly admitted it.

As we have stated in many previous talks and books, we feel, in our opinion, that the first nine steps put the alcoholic "on the program." Each one is taken completely once and for all, although we must *never* forget step one; many A.A.'s remind themselves of it every day.

However, steps ten, eleven, and twelve are *continuing* steps—day in and day out, or week in or week out, or as often as our *honest* conscience dictates their repetition. We repeat the personal inventory, the prayers and meditations, and the twelfth step activities, as often as we honestly think we should.

Step ten, which we are now considering, is a "personal inventory"—and inventory of what? How good we are? How often we have succeeded? Or how often we have failed? We rather think it should especially look for only one thing: how *willing* are we. After all that is all that God asks from us: for approval, for sanction!

Let's look more closely. If we constantly search for our successes, does He oppose of His own work? He gave these to us! It was His work! And if we continually look for our failures, do we fill ourselves with remorse and self-blame? He did not do these wrongs, but He *did* permit them. Now where do we come in. How does an inventory get His approval? We have His approval and His sanction as long *as we are willing—trying*. Our will is all that is ours, and it is willingness alone that is sure of His *sanction!*

"And when we were wrong promptly admitted it." As we said above God does not approve sin or wrong, but He does approve our willingness, in face of failure and wrongs and sin. So, here in our admission, we *again* become *willing*. Again we have His approval; His *sanction!* And sanction is sanctity.

11) *Sought through prayer and meditation to improve our conscious contact with God as we understood Him praying only for the knowledge of His Will for us and the power to carry it out.*

Behold the very essence of perfection! The knowledge of the Will of God and the power to carry it out!

Many churchmen criticized A.A. in years gone by, saying A.A. was unacceptable to Christians because it was a merely 'naturalistic' program. There can be little doubt that such people never read the Twelve Steps, especially the one we are considering now; the eleventh step. In fact some years ago, a very outstanding clergyman made the statement to us: "A Catholic should not partake in the A.A. program, because it is purely a naturalistic one." It took some time to get an honest answer from him when I queried him on whether he had ever read the twelve steps. In staccato, he kept saying: yes, yes, yes, yes, as he thumbed through a sheath of papers on his desk. Finally, we, in a louder voice, stopped him asking very emphatically, "Did you ever read the twelve steps or not?" To this he very begrudgingly said, "Well, no—but I know what they are!"

It was here that we took out the big A.A. Book and read the eleventh step very clearly and slowly, and remarked: "How can anyone read this step and miss the Finger of God in it? Naturalistic? If any member would ever achieve this step perfectly *every day*— their name would probably be Therese! Of Lisieux! For all in all, perfection, even heroic sanctity *must* be brought about by perfect union of wills—the human and the Divine. And when that union is uninterrupted and constant—that is heroic sanctity." He agreed!

However, in A.A. and in ordinary practice, this does not happen. We do not work the eleventh step perfectly nor uninterruptedly nor permanently. We only *grow*—along spiritual lines. But God knows the weakness of our nature. And our honest try again and again breeds willingness to eventually join those two wills together—and God approves, He sanctions our willingness—and that is sanctity, simple though it may be!

The prayer and meditation in this step brings God more and more into our conscious living; the praying for knowledge of His Will for us and the power to carry it out enables us to know His Will for us so that we may join our will with *His*, and in the joining He will give also the power and the strength to carry it out. And God approves, He still sanctions not the *failure*, but *us*. So you ain't a saint? Only if you do not honestly *try*; only if you are not *willing*. And should you be one of those who are not willing, all you have to do is to repeat and repeat and repeat: "God make me willing," which He will. Otherwise, if we do not even try, or ask for willingness, we will in all probability one of these days begin all over again on step one!

So, here in step eleven: let us seek, let us ask, let us try, and we will be "approved."

12) *Having had a spiritual awakening as a result of these steps, we tried to carry this message to alcoholics, and to practice these principles in all our affairs.*

First of all in step twelve we have a "spiritual awakening." We *awaken* and we *begin* to see all things in the light of God's Will not men's. The most important thing we *begin* to realize is the value of spiritual things; the effectiveness of God's help; and the necessity of our will submitting to Him—the joining of wills. We have finally realized once and for all that we are *men approved*; that we have God's approval.

1) *To carry the message to alcoholics, and*

2) *That God's Will for us is to practice these principles in all of our affairs.*

May we quote from a little two-page pamphlet distributed by many A.A. groups here and there:

"God in His Wisdom has selected you and all A.A.'s to be the purveyors of His Goodness. In selecting them through whom to bring about this phenomenon, He went not to the mighty, the famous or to the brilliant. He went to the sick, to cast-offs, to the unfortunate—He went right to the alcoholic, the so-called weakling of this world.'"

"Well might He have said to us—into your weak and feeble hands I have entrusted a power beyond estimate, which when used for other alcoholics directly returns to you in strengthening your own sobriety. This was not given to some of the most learned of your fellowmen. Not to scientists, not to statesmen, not to wives or mothers. Not even to your closest friends and loved ones has this gift been given—the ability of identifying with and of healing the sick alcoholic while at the same time increasing your own quality and length of sobriety."

"It must be used unselfishly...because it is the ladder you are to use to ascend the rungs toward spiritual perfection and the fulfillment of My Will both for you and for them. Through A.A. you will eventually join them all with Mine, held together for all eternity by this bond of perfection in charity."

"You were selected because you were the outcasts, the weak ones of this world, and the long experience of alcoholism in yourself would make you keenly alert to the cries of distress that come from the lonely, dying hearts of alcoholics everywhere. So, keep ever in mind the admission you made when you entered the ranks of A.A., namely that you are powerless, then, now and forever and that it will always be dependent upon your *willingness* to turn your life and your will into My keeping. For it is in doing this you gain My approval, My sanction—and *your* sobriety."

And what are the principles of A.A. for which we daily seek approval? They are many; they are all in these Twelve Steps—they are, as we just quoted above: "The rungs of the ladder you are to use to ascend to and gradually grow toward spiritual perfection and the fulfillment of My Will...."

Approval!

Sanction!

Sanctity!

LET'S AT LEAST BEGIN

The entire working of A.A. wherein the Power of *God as we understand Him,* not only reclaims, but rehabilitates and perfects, is beautifully expressed in the poem:

The Old Violin

"Twas battered, scarred, and the auctioneer
Thought it scarcely worth the while
To waste his time on the old violin
But he held it up with a smile.
"What am I bidden, good people," he cried
"Who'll start the bidding for me?
A dollar, a dollar, now two, only two;
Two dollars, and who'll make it three?
Three dollars once, three dollars twice;
Going for three?" but no
From the room far back, a gray haired man
Came forward and picked up the bow.
Then wiping the dust from the old violin
And tightening up the strings,
He played a melody pure and sweet,
As sweet as an angel sings.
The music ceased and the auctioneer

> With a voice that was quiet and low
> Said, "What am I bid for the old violin?"
> And he held it up with the bow.
> "A thousand dollars and who'll make it two?'
> Two thousand, and who'll make it three?
> Three thousand once, three thousand twice;
> And going and gone," said he.
> We don't quite understand
> What changed its worth?"
> Swift came the reply:
> "The touch of the master's hand."
> And many a man with life out of tune
> And battered and torn with sin,
> Is auctioned cheap to the thoughtless crowd
> Much like the old violin.
> A mess of pottage, a glass of wine,
> A game, and he travels on.
> He is going once, and going twice;
> He's going and almost gone,
> But then the Master comes and the foolish crowd
> Never can quite understand
> The worth of a soul, and the change that is wrought
> By the touch of the Master's Hand."

Throughout history no one was more indicted, more scorned and called more hopeless by the passing crowd than the alcoholic. Doctors, lawyers, judges, clergymen and all agreed again and again that the alcoholic was the one "hopeless" case. But then came A.A. and 300,000 "hopeless" cases have been restored to sobriety and society—'by the touch of the Master's Hand: *God as we understood Him.*

In the preceding pages of this little booklet, we have seen how these alcoholics can and have ascended twelve steps—joined to the Will of God—and instead of cast-offs, became *approved*—sanctioned not by men, nor by you nor by us, but by God.

But before we proceed any farther along, let's stop a moment and go back in history of the not too distant past when a fellow by the name of John F. Kennedy was sworn in as President of the United States. It is not our intention to be in any way politically entangled, but in his Inaugural Address he made a statement which has remained very firmly in our memory. He related the various proposals for his administration, and then added: "These things will not be accomplished in an hour, or a day, or in weeks, or months—perhaps not even in years: but

Let's at least begin!"

So may we now repeat all of the foregoing in our booklet and repeat these words again: "We may not achieve all these things we spoke of (including *sanctity*) in an hour, nor a day, or a week, or a month—maybe not for years—in fact, maybe not fully until death or even into eternity, *but at least, let's begin!*

We may be able to *"dry up"* in an hour or a day, or days—but total sobriety, total sanctity comes to us as everything else in life by *growth*. As the A.A. Book says: "We are willing to grow along spiritual lines..." And we will be doing just that not only for days, or months, or years but for a lifetime! So *let's at least begin!*

The brilliant principle which A.A. insists on—to the new (and old) members—over and over again is: "Easy does it." "You didn't get drunk overnight, and you won't reach full sobriety overnight"—in fact it will take, maybe, months or years, *"But let's at least begin!"*

Also in A.A. the spiritual life, we "are willing to grow"—not for an hour, nor a day, nor months, nor even years, but until death—but one step, one day at a time. Easy does it! Let us not be fooled by the A.A. Book's statement into taking only half of it: "We are not saints—period." Me a saint? Never. Let's read it all: "We are not saints...we are *willing to grow along spiritual lines*. And so just as a seed of corn will eventually become a stalk of corn if it *grows*: so will everyone, even the biggest sinner may someday become a saint if he or she is willing to *grow* along spiritual lines. The A.A. philosophy tells us that we "are willing to grow along spiritual lines," and by this fact tells us that the ultimate for all A.A.'s is sanctity. And as we have read all through this booklet, it is very simple, but a one-day-at-a time process always and everywhere; in all things good, bad and indifferent, it is solely dependent upon and achieved by the obtaining of the approval of God *for us*—as we understand His Will in our *honest* conscience.

Is this difficult? Hardly, but it may be lengthy, and it may not be achieved as a matter of habit in an hour, or a day, or a week or even a lifetime. But to all in A.A. who make an honest effort to grow, it will be achieved at least in eternity forever.

So, let's at least begin!

All in A.A. may very readily and efficiently carry this all into many phases of living:

1) *In our homes—the family.* Those problems which seem to pile up so high in families—entailing mother, father and children. We may not solve them all in an hour, or a day, or a month or for years— *but let's at least begin!*

And speaking of problems, we believe that it would be a good idea to reprint here a statement from our Golden Book of Excuses, which will very dramatically emphasize, we hope, the tremendous importance of the phrase we are meditating upon, not only in the pursuit of sanctity, but in all problems:

"On the plains of desolation there bleaches the bones of *countless millions* who at the very dawn of victory, sat down to wait—and waiting—died!"

So let's at least begin!

2) *In our social activities—in and out of A.A., charity is the bond of perfection.* But let us not forget that true charity is also willingness

to love our neighbor: good, bad or indifferent; drunk or sober, sinner or saint (of whom you say there ain't!) Liking is emotional; loving is *willing*. In fact if we take the greatest of all the commandments we will find that we must *love* our neighbor as ourselves. And love, real love, true love is in the *will*. "To men of good *will*;" or as our good protestant friends might also say "Good *will* to men." Never forget sin, virtue, love and sanctity—are *always* in the *will*!

So we meet lots and lots of alcoholics in A.A. Let's have *good will* to all. Then God will approve. It may be days, or weeks, or years until we actually meet them all—but *let's at least begin*—today, by willing! Let's trade our sanction of them for God's sanction of us!

3) *Giving sobriety to another.* We, many times will not be able to do so—on the first call—in a day, nor a week, nor a month—maybe not for years; But *let's at least begin!* Then some day, in God's time and way, we will *"make it,"* and in the meantime *you* will be staying sober. How many have *slipped* for years and years—but finally make it! Many after five, ten, fifteen years!

Every attempt of ours, every try, every endeavor is known to God—and He approves your *attempts* to sober up others giving proof in the sobriety given to you; and maybe He does and maybe He doesn't explicitly approve the other guy's or gal's repeated slipping; but *He does permit them!* He could, being God, stop them; but He doesn't. And as we have just mentioned above, eventually to many of them He does give sobriety, and a very solid brand—along with His sanction! Approve their slipping? Hmmmmmmm, maybe! Let us recall: *"a cross of sin!"* Could be!

So let's at least begin!

4) *The Twelve Steps.* We hear much discussion in A.A. circles about these steps. How should they be taken, when should they be taken, how much in detail should they be taken, and especially how soon should twelfth step calls be taken.

Let's answer all very shortly:

How should they be taken?

By being willing to do so honestly in our own way—so, *let's at least begin!*

One to twelve—should they all be taken; in what order? Again, simply by being honestly willing to take them—as you *honestly* think is best *for you. So, let's at least begin!*

How much in detail should each be taken? In being willing to do so in just that detail which you are honestly convinced is necessary for *you*! So, let's get going. *Let's at least begin!*

How soon should they all be taken?

Just as soon as you are ready and willing! And may we admonish all—never force your self to take a step *against* either your *will* or honest *conviction*. In reality this is dishonest. God does *not* approve. But we should keep an *open* mind! So, *let's at least begin!*

How soon should a new member take twelfth step calls? There is much disagreement among the groups as to the best answer for this one. But whenever they start, *God will approve!* And He will, in fact go along on the call! So why not take Him along—by prayer, instead of figuring out what *we* are going to say. And our own personal opinion is that the new member should make a twelfth step call—the sooner the better. What has he to offer so soon? Well he has a few days or weeks sobriety more than the one who called! In fact sometimes we feel a long time sober fellow or gal making a call might even 'scare' the jittery, shaky prospect. Fifteen years!?

So, *let's at least begin*—the sooner the better. This will at least keep the new member sober. Twelfth step calls are the instrument of our sobriety; God is the source!

> Of all sobriety!
> Of all sanctity!
> *So, let's at least begin!*

What was that we quoted in the very beginning of our meditation on Sanctity?

Me a saint?
You know I ain't—
And could never, never be:
What's that you say?
"A man approved?
Today?
By God;
Not men
Or even me!
No matter what I am;
Or will ever, ever be?
You mean that I . . . .
Again—let's read on
And this time really see;
One in the flesh
Who did receive—approval
And sanctity:

It is a quotation from a recent letter received by us after the death of a priest member of Alcoholics Anonymous. For obvious reasons we omit the name, place and date. Its message also is quite obvious. We, ourselves, are truly grateful in playing a small part in Father X's sobriety. The letter was written to us by a lay member of A.A.

"Dear Father:

A.A. lost a wonderful member last week when Father X died. Death came rather quickly although Father suffered greatly the last two weeks. A High Mass was sung yesterday for him at his funeral. The Bishop gave one of the finest sermons I have ever heard. He started it with the Serenity Prayer and then spoke of Father's devotion to A.A. and how he had found the fullness of his vocation through A.A. In closing he expressed the wish that all bishops and priests could have witnessed Father's death. There were many priests and many non-Catholics present. I have attended a lot of funerals, but never have been so deeply affected. A.A. certainly lost a wonderful member, a wonderful man last week—and so did the Priesthood...."

> *"Father X," truly*
> *'A man approved'—*
> *By God....*
> *Now a Saint*
> *In reality:*
> *In God's Eternity!"*

So—let's you and me, and you and you and you and all

> At *least begin—today!*

                Imprimatur.
                ✠ PAUL C. SCHULTE D.D.
                      Archbishop of Indianapolis
                March 24, 1967

THE TWELVE STEPS

1. We admitted we were powerless over alcohol—that our lives had become unmanageable.

2. Came to believe that a Power greater than ourselves could restore us to sanity.

3. Made a decision to turn our will and our lives over to the care of God *as we understood Him.*

4. Made a searching and fearless moral inventory of ourselves.

5. Admitted to God, to ourselves, and to another human being the exact nature of our wrongs.

6. Were entirely ready to have God remove all these defects of character.

7. Humbly asked Him to remove our shortcomings.

8. Made a list of all persons we had harmed, and became willing to make amends to them all.

9. Made direct amends to such people wherever possible, except when to do so would injure them or others.

10. Continued to take personal inventory and when we were wrong promptly admitted it.

11. Sought through prayer and meditation to improve our conscious contact with God *as we understood Him,* praying only for knowledge of His will for us and the power to carry that out.

12. Having had a spiritual experience as the result of these steps, we tried to carry this message to alcoholics, and to practice these principles in all our affairs.

About Hazelden Publishing

As part of the Hazelden Betty Ford Foundation, Hazelden Publishing offers both cutting-edge educational resources and inspirational books. Our print and digital works help guide individuals in treatment and recovery, and their loved ones. Professionals who work to prevent and treat addiction also turn to Hazelden Publishing for evidence-based curricula, digital content solutions, and videos for use in schools, treatment programs, correctional programs, and electronic health records systems. We also offer training for implementation of our curricula.

Through published and digital works, Hazelden Publishing extends the reach of healing and hope to individuals, families, and communities affected by addiction and related issues.

For more information about Hazelden publications,
please call **800-328-9000**
or visit us online at **hazelden.org/bookstore.**